bubblefacts...
SCIENCE WORLD

miles KELLY
PUBLISHING

First published in 2004 by
Miles Kelly Publishing Ltd
Bardfield Centre, Great Bardfield, Essex, CM7 4SL

2 4 6 8 10 9 7 5 3 1

Editorial Director:
Anne Marshall

Senior Editor:
Belinda Gallagher

Editorial Assistant:
Lisa Clayden

Designer:
Debbie Meekcoms

Cartoons:
Mark Davis

Production:
Estela Boulton

ISBN 1–84236–435–9

Printed in China

British Library Cataloguing–in–Publication Data
A catalogue record for this book is available from the British Library

Indexer: Jane Parker

www.mileskelly.net
info@mileskelly.net

Contents

Science world

making life easier

Science is everywhere. All the machines we use, from toasters to mobile phones, are the result of scientific discoveries. Houses, skyscrapers, bridges and rockets are built using science. Our knowledge of medicine, light and nature comes from science. Our whole world relies upon science and technology.

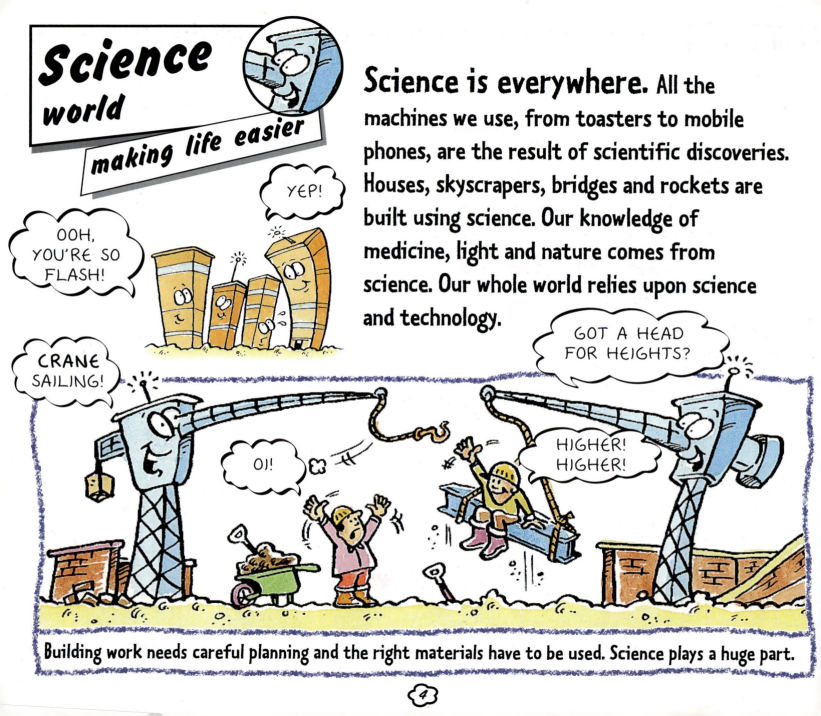

Building work needs careful planning and the right materials have to be used. Science plays a huge part.

Fumes from traffic can create lots of pollution, especially in cities. This can lead to poor air quality and damage to the environment. Scientists are constantly researching new, cleaner fuels and methods of transport.

A ramp is a simple machine called an inclined plane. It's easier to walk up a ramp than to jump straight to the top.

I'M DRIVEN TO DISTRACTION!

ZZZOOOOOOmm!

PLANE SAILING!

HALLOO!

In a big city, almost every vehicle, building, machine and gadget is based on science and technology.

Flaming science
hot hot hot!

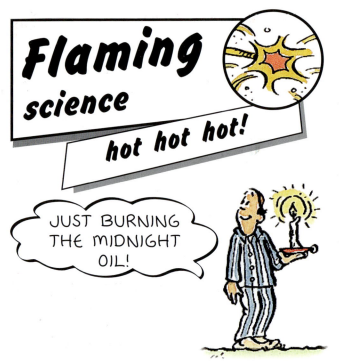

JUST BURNING THE MIDNIGHT OIL!

The science of heat is important in all kinds of ways. Heat is used for cooking, boiling water and keeping homes warm. Engines burn fuel to power vehicles, such as planes, cars, trucks and rockets. Heat is also used in many factory processes such as making steel and shaping plastics.

A firework burns as an explosive, with heat, light and sound. This burning process is called combustion.

Heat moves in three ways. Conduction is when a hot object transfers some heat to a cooler one, such as a spoon in a hot drink. Radiation is the way the Sun's warmth moves through space. Convection is when heat moves through liquids and gases. Some of the liquid or gas takes in heat, gets lighter and rises. Think of the 'wavy' hot air over a candle.

Temperature is the amount of heat in a substance. It is usually measured in degrees Celsius (°C).

Waves
of sound
noisy science

The science of sound is called acoustics. Sounds are like invisible waves in the air. The peak (highest point) of the wave is where a region of air is squashed under high pressure. The trough (lowest point) of the wave is a region where air is expanded under low pressure.

Sound is measured in decibels (dB). A watch ticking is 10 dB. A jet plane taking off is 120 dB.

Sound waves travel 330 metres a second. They bounce off hard surfaces and the returning waves are called echoes.

Loudspeakers change electrical signals into sounds. The signals in a wire pass through a coil inside the speaker. This turns the coil into a magnet, which pushes and pulls against another magnet. The pushing and pulling make a cone vibrate, which sends sound waves into the air.

FANCY A RUMBLE?

PERSONALITY CLASH!

PUT A SOCK IN IT!

TWEET TWEET!

...ounds are high- or low-pitched and measured in Hertz. Thunder is low-pitched. Bird song is high-pitched.

Lighting our lives

the speed of light

Almost everything you do needs light and the science of light, which is called optics. Light is a form of energy that you can see. It is made up of tiny waves of electricity and magnetism. About 2000 of these waves laid end to end would stretch across this fullstop.

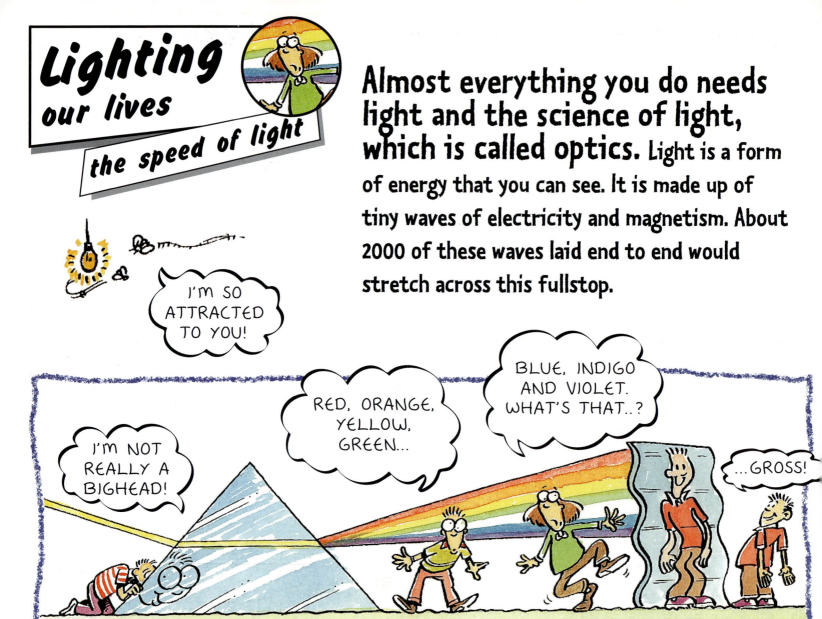

When white light is passed through a glass triangle, it splits into the seven colours of the rainbow.

Like sound, light bounces off surfaces that are very smooth. This is called reflection. A mirror is smooth, hard and flat. When you look at it you can see your reflection.

Light is the fastest thing in the Universe. It travels through space at 300,000 kilometres a second – seven times around the world in less than a second!

I'M SO CURVY.

SUCH BIG TEETH...

...AND HAIRY LEGS!

Mirrors and lenses are special parts in light-using gadgets such as cameras, telescopes and binoculars.

Engine power

get fired up!

Can you imagine if you had to walk everywhere instead of travelling by car? Engines are machines that do work for us. Fuel is a substance that has chemical energy stored in it. This energy is released as heat by burning or exploding the fuel in an engine.

Air and petrol are ignited in car engines. This pushes a piston to move the gears, which turns the wheels.

Engines in modern tractors are extremely powerful. This lets the tractor operate ploughs and other machinery with ease.

A jet engine mixes air and kerosene and sets fire to it for one long, continuous roaring explosion. Incredibly hot gases blast out of the back of the engine. These push the plane forward with great force.

CHUG CHUG CHUG CHUG!

TRACTORS! I HATE THEM! I'M SOO LATE!

SLOW AND STEADY...

In diesel engines, such as in trains, air and diesel are squashed so that they become hot and explode.

Amazing atoms

small is beautiful

Atoms are the smallest parts of a substance. They are so tiny, even one billion atoms would be too small to see. Inside an atom are even smaller parts. These are sub-atomic particles and there are three main kinds: electrons, protons and neutrons. The nucleus (centre) of an atom is made up of protons and neutrons.

READY? LET'S SPLIT!

HERE'S ONE I MADE EARLIER.

I STILL CAN'T SEE IT!

LOOK! AN ATOMIC MODEL.

Parts of an atom give substances their features. A hydrogen atom has one proton, making it explosive.

It's hard to imagine that atoms are so small. A grain of sand, smaller than this 'o' contains at least 100 billion billion atoms. If atoms could be made bigger so that each one becomes as big as a pinhead, the grain of sand would be 2 kilometres high.

About 100 years ago, people thought that electrons in an atom were spread out, like raisins in a raisin pudding!

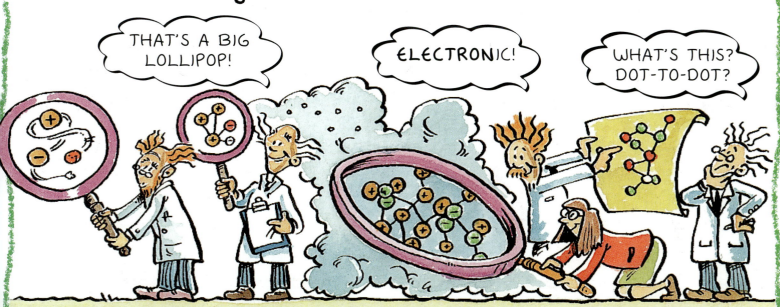

THAT'S A BIG LOLLIPOP!

ELECTRONIC!

WHAT'S THIS? DOT-TO-DOT?

Electrons whiz around the nucleus of an atom. They jump from atom to atom when electricity flows.

Magic magnets

pulling power!

Without any magnets there'd be no loudspeakers, motors, or computers. Magnetism is an invisible force to do with the way atoms (tiny particles) and electrons (even smaller particles) line up and move. Most magnetic substances contain iron. Iron makes up a large part of the metallic substance steel, so steel is also magnetic.

I'VE PULLED!

WE HAD THIS INSTANT ATTRACTION!

Z Z Z I I I...

A magnet is a piece of iron or steel that has its electrons and atoms lined up. This creates a magnetic fie

A magnet has a north and a south pole. The north pole pushes away (repels) the north pole of another magnet. Two south poles also repel each other. A north and a south pole pull together (attract). Both magnetic poles attract any substance that contains iron, such as a nail or a screw.

When electricity flows through a metal wire, it creates a weak magnetic field around it. If the wire is wrapped into a coil, the magnetism grows stronger. This is called an electromagnet. When the electricity goes off, the magnetism does too. Some electromagnets are so strong, they can lift entire cars.

.N N N N N N N N G!

IN YOUR DREAMS!

GOT THE NEEDLE?

I HAVE A MAGNETIC PERSONALITY!

As Earth spins in space, its iron centre becomes a magnet. This is what makes compass needles move.

Bright sparks

flick the switch!

Electricity is an important form of energy. At a power station, fuel such as coal or oil is burnt to heat water into high-pressure steam. The steam spins a turbine, which turns coils of wire nearby into powerful magnets. This makes electricity flow in the coils.

YOU'RE A LIVE WIRE!

COUCH POTATO? ME? NEVER!

BLAH! BLAH!

RING! RING!

Power stations supply electricity to thousands of homes. Electricity enters homes through a meter.

Washing machines use electricity. They wash and rinse clothes, then spin them to force out the water.

In fact we use electricity to power hundreds of machines, from food blenders to toasters and irons!

Amazing airports

into the air!

Without science we would have to walk everywhere. There are many methods of transport, but none gets us further faster than flying. Modern airports are huge and can stretch for several miles. There is a constant flow of planes taking off and landing.

Jetw

Jetways are extending walkways that stretch out like telescopic fingers right to the door of a plane. Their supports move along wheeled trolleys driven by electric motors. In the air, planes are tracked on radar screens by air traffic controllers. They talk to pilots by radio. Beacons send out radio signals, giving direction and distance from the airport.

Hundreds of staff are needed to make sure that an airport runs smoothly and safely.

Passenger terminal

Underground trains take passengers to and from the terminal

Planes are tracked by radar. The radar screens show each aircraft as a blip, with its flight number.

Making sounds...
...and pictures

The air is full of sounds and waves we cannot hear without the right machine. Radio waves are a form of electrical and magnetic energy, just like heat and light waves, microwaves and X-rays. These electromagnetic waves travel at an equal speed – the speed of light.

Radio and TV programmes may be sent out as radio waves from a transmitter on the ground.

You can listen to radio waves in space, but not underwater. Radio waves travel easily through space, but can hardly pass through water.

In a TV set, the pattern of radio waves is changed into electrical signals. Some make sound in the speakers and others go to the screen to make pictures. The screen is at the front of a glass container called a tube. At the back of this, a 'gun' fires streams of electrons at coloured dots called phosphors. When electrons hit the dots, the phosphors glow to make a picture.

IS ANYONE OUT THERE?

I'M A WIDE, WIDE SCREEN!

...metimes waves can be broadcast by satellites in space. Programmes can also arrive by laser, as on cable TV.

Computer crazy

wafers and chips!

Computers are really amazing machines. Instructions are given to a computer by various means. These include typing on a keyboard, inserting a disc, using a joystick or games board, or by linking to a camera, scanner or another computer.

Can you believe it?

The World Wide Web has more than 3000 million pages of information.

HI!

IS IT SERIOUS, DOC?

I'M AFRAID SO... A REALLY NASTY VIRUS.

Some computers can be voice controlled. Computers can get viruses – files that cause them damage.

A computer's 'brain' is a tiny microchip. It receives information, carries out work and gives results.

The results usually go to the monitor, or screen. They can also go to a printer or be stored on CD.

What's it made of?

magic materials

Choosing the right substance for a task is part of materials science. Substances can be divided into groups, with the biggest being metals such as iron, copper, silver and gold. Most metals are hard and strong, and they carry heat and electricity well. They are used where materials must be tough and long-lasting.

Plastic is a useful material, made from crude oil (petroleum). It is long-lasting and not affected by damp.

Ceramics are materials based on clay or other substances dug from the earth. They can be shaped and dried, like a clay bowl. They can also be fired – baked in a hot oven called a kiln. This makes them hard and long-lasting, but brittle and prone to cracks. Ceramics resist heat and electricity well.

A racing car has many thousands of parts and uses lots of different materials. The main body of the car is made from carbon fibre, a light but very strong material. The tyres are made from thick, tough rubber to withstand high speeds, while the engine has to be light, but able to produce about ten times more power than an ordinary car.

WHOOOOSSHHH!

TOP GLASS!

HANG ON A MINUTE!

AND THEY'RE OFF!

Glass is made from limestone and sand. When heated it becomes a liquid, which sets hard as it cools.

Science, naturally!

the living world

Scientists study the effects of science on the natural world.

They look at animals, plants, rocks and soil to try to understand more about nature. One of the most complicated types of science is ecology. Ecologists look at how animals and plants live. If the balance of nature is damaged, ecologists help to find out why.

Ecologists sometimes trap animals briefly to study them. They look at how pollution affects them.

Almost everything we make or do affects animals and plants. Factories, power stations and traffic can be especially harmful as they give off chemicals that spread in the air, and seep into soil and water.

Can you believe it?

Some animals, such as whales and birds, use the Earth's natural magnetism to migrate, or travel around.

Some animals are fitted with radio collars so they can be tracked. Cameras capture how animals hunt.

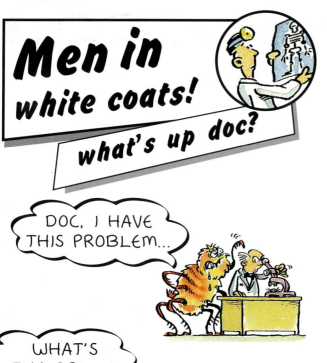

Men in white coats!
what's up doc?

Medicine is one of the biggest areas of science. Medical scientists work to produce better drugs and machines for use by doctors. They also carry out scientific research to find out how people can stay healthy and look at new ways of preventing disease.

Lasers are used to treat eye problems. An endoscope is like a flexible telescope to see inside the body.

Muscles and nerves produce pulses of electricity. Pads on the skin pick these up and display them as wavy lines on a screen. An ECG (electro-cardiogram) machine shows the heart beating. An EEG (electro-encephalogram) shows nerve signals flashing around the brain.

As the body works, electrical signals can be picked up by machines to see how well it is functioning.

Index